UNITI

JOKES OF

AMERICA

To my mom, Donna, for saying, "You should be a writer!"
—C. S. O.

To Rose and our kids...five people whose
funny bones are as big as their hearts.
—A. K.

ISBN 0-439-69732-8

12 11 10 9 8 7 6 5 4 3 2   6 7 8 9 10/0

Printed in the U.S.A.
First Printing, April 2005

UNITED JOKES OF AMERICA

By Alan Katz and Caissie St. Onge

Illustrated by Mike Lester

SCHOLASTIC INC.

New York   Toronto   London   Auckland   Sydney
Mexico City   New Delhi   Hong Kong   Buenos Aires

Introduction

If you think the last two words
of "The Star Spangled Banner"
are "play ball!"...

If you're convinced that New Jersey
is something you buy at the
start of football season...

If you're studying American history
and geography and your report
card is covered with grades from
"C to shining C" (or D!)...

WE'RE WITH YOU!

(Because we thought all that, too,
before we decided to do this book!)

But now we know better...and we've found
a ton of funnies in the states from A to Z

(well, really, from A to W, since there
are no states that start with a Z—or
for that matter a B, E, J, Q, X, or Y)!

And we've even unearthed some actual laws
from state records...they're outdated but hilarious,
and fortunately no one's enforcing them now!
So get ready to tour the fabulous 50 states with us
...and get ready to laugh...

...at the United Jokes of America!

Alabama

ABBREVIATION: *AL*

STATE CAPITAL: *Montgomery*

NICKNAME: *Heart of Dixie*

FLOWER: *Camellia*

BIRD: *Yellowhammer*

TREE: *Southern Longleaf Pine*

SONG: *"Alabama"*

ENTERED UNION: *December 14, 1819*

A FAMOUS ALABAMIAN: *Condoleeza Rice*

Why did the **Alabama** carpenter's house fall apart?

Because he used a yellowhammer

(The yellowhammer is Alabama's state bird.)

What is the favorite song of **Alabama** cotton farmers?

Pop Goes the Weevil

(Weevils are insects that destroy cotton crops.)

What Alabama military station makes all soldiers shake in their boots?

Fort Payne

Q: Did you know that the first rocket to put humans on the moon was built by Alabamians?

A: When they were done, did they go out to launch?

What did the elephant from Italy say to his Alabama dentist?

Help—my Tuscaloosa!

What do you call an orphaned baby deer from this state?

Alabambi

What do you call Alabama's official state nut when it has a negative attitude?

A pecan't

What do you call it when the University of Alabama's baseball team has the same score as their opponent?

Crimson Tied

(The University of Alabama's sports teams are known as "The Crimson Tide," and their battle cry is "Roll Tide!")

Why should Emeril like visiting Huntsville?

Because it's in Ala-BAM-a!

Alaska

ABBREVIATION: *AK*

STATE CAPITAL: *Juneau*

NICKNAME: *Last Frontier*

FLOWER: *Forget-Me-Not*

BIRD: *Willow Ptarmigan*

TREE: *Sitka Spruce*

SONG: *"Alaska's Flag"*

ENTERED UNION: *January 3, 1959*

A FAMOUS ALASKAN: *Jewel*

Why do people like to borrow money in Alaska?

Because they have Fairbanks

How does an Eskimo fix his house when it breaks?

He ig-glues it

What food do you get when you put a piece of glacier between two buns?

Iceburger

What does an Alaskan do when he bumps into the supermarket shelf?

Ketchikan

How old do you have to be to park your ship in Alaska?

Anchor-age

Is it possible to find gold in Alaska?

Yukon if you look hard!

What did one bowhead whale say to the other bowhead whale?

STOP BLUBBERING!

What do you call it when an Eskimo's pants fall down?

Northern exposure

Arizona

ABBREVIATION: *AZ*

STATE CAPITAL: *Phoenix*

NICKNAME: *Grand Canyon State*

FLOWER: *Blossom of the Saguaro Cactus*

BIRD: *Cactus Wren*

TREE: *Paloverde*

SONG: *"Arizona"*

ENTERED UNION: *February 14, 1912*

A FAMOUS ARIZONAN:
Frank Lloyd Wright

What would a Saguaro plant wear to a formal event?

A cac-tie

What do Arizona ghost towns Tombstone, Ruby, Gillette, and Gunsight all have in common?

They've all got lots of spirit

Where should you visit if you don't like the Painted Desert?

The Wall-Papered Desert

What does the little canyon call it's mother's mother?

The GRANDMA *Canyon*

What happened when a ghost visited an Arizona forest?

The trees were petrified

In Arizona, what gift could you find for a baby herpetologist?

A rattlesnake

What did the kid say to his Arizonan mother when she asked who was the nicest lady in the whole state?

You, ma!

Why does the **Arizona** tree frog make such a good friend?

It'll always go out on a limb for you

Ya Know What?

Four Corners is a spot in the United States where you can put each of your hands and feet in four states at the same time (Arizona, New Mexico, Utah, Colorado).

15

Arkansas

ABBREVIATION: AR

STATE CAPITAL: Little Rock

NICKNAME: Natural State

FLOWER: Apple Blossom

BIRD: Mockingbird

TREE: Pine

SONG: "Arkansas"

ENTERED UNION: June 15, 1836

A FAMOUS ARKANSAN: President Bill Clinton

What do you use to cut wood in this state?

An Arkan-saw

What kind of music does a tiny band play?

Little Rock

What do you call someone who packs gemstones in boxes?

Crater of Diamonds

Who was **Arkansas**'s most valuable singer?

Johnny Cash

Q: Did you enter the World's Championship Duck Calling Contest in Stuttgart?

A: No. No ducks would give me their phone number!

HOW DO YOU FEEL ABOUT THE DIAMOND BEING **ARKANSAS**'s OFFICIAL STATE GEM?
I don't **karat** all!

What do you call a pile of periodicals so high you could climb it?

Mount Magazine

What happens to nervous honeybees?
They get hives

(The honeybee is Arkansas's state insect.)

California

ABBREVIATION: *CA*

STATE CAPITAL: *Sacramento*

NICKNAME: *Golden State*

FLOWER: *Golden Poppy*

BIRD: *California Valley Quail*

TREE: *California Redwood*

SONG: *"I Love You, California"*

ENTERED UNION: *September 9, 1850*

A FAMOUS CALIFORNIAN: *Tiger Woods*

Where should you visit in California if you're very, very tired?

Napa Valley

What do you call it when you fall on the beach and scrape your knee?

A Malibu-boo

What state are you in if King Midas touches you?

The Golden State

What do you call it when your mom makes you carry her twenty-pound purse?

The Mother Lode

(During the gold rush, everyone wanted to hit the Mother Lode—it meant you'd found a whole lot of gold!)

Q: Did you know Fresno is the raisin capital of the world?

A: Yeah, I heard it through the grapevine

In **California**, where would a hungry giant pour his breakfast cereal?

The Hollywood Bowl

Why do single people hang out in Coachella Valley?

Because it's the Date Capital of the World

HE: Did you know there are more cars than people in Los Angeles?

SHE: Leave me alone, I have to go park my sister

Colorado

ABBREVIATION: *CO*

STATE CAPITAL: *Denver*

NICKNAME: *Centennial State*

FLOWER: *Rocky Mountain Columbine*

BIRD: *Lark Bunting*

TREE: *Colorado Blue Spruce*

SONG: *"Where the Columbines Grow"*

ENTERED UNION: *August 1, 1876*

A FAMOUS COLORADAN: *John Kerry*

What's the saddest tree in Colorado?

The blue spruce

What's in Colorado, full of money, and good after you eat onions?

The U.S. Mint

What did they call it when Lt. Zebulon Pike snuck a look at his gifts before his birthday?

Pike's Peek

Q: **What do you think about Grand Mesa, the world's largest flattop mountain?**

A: **It has no point**

What's the heaviest city in Colorado?

Leadville

If Cupid moved to Colorado, what town would he choose?

Loveland

What did the Rocky Ford melon say to his girlfriend?

I want to get married, but we cantaloupe

What do you call bald eagles that sing hip-hop?

Rap-tors

Connecticut

ABBREVIATION: *CT*

STATE CAPITOL: *Hartford*

NICKNAMES: *Constitution State, Nutmeg State*

FLOWER: *Mountain Laurel*

BIRD: *American Robin*

TREE: *White Oak*

SONG: *"Yankee Doodle"*

RATIFIED THE CONSTITUTION: *January 9, 1788*

A FAMOUS "NUTMEGGER": *Ralph Nader*

What do you call it when someone from Connecticut scribbles a picture?

Yankee Doodle

What do you get when you cross writer Samuel Clemens with a steam engine?

A choo-choo Twain

(Mark Twain continues to be one of America's favorite writers. Have you read **Huckleberry Finn**?)

Where should all the fortune-tellers live in Connecticut?

Mystic Seaport

Have you decided if you're going to visit the WWF headquarters in Stamford?

No, I've been wrestling with it all week

What do you call a spice that's yummy in apple pie, or your Aunt Margaret when she acts crazy?

Nut-Meg

(Besides being the Constitution State, Connecticut is also known as the Nutmeg State!)

Where's the best place in Connecticut to get a hero sandwich?

The Navy Sub Base

What would you say if I asked you to move to my house in Greenwich?

Are you trying to Conn me?

Did you know that Connecticut does not have a state fair?

No fair? No fair!

Ya Know What?

In Colonial times, residents of New Haven, Connecticut, used carved pumpkins as guides for haircuts, earning them the nickname "Pumpkin Heads."

Delaware

ABBREVIATION: *DE*

STATE CAPITAL: *Dover*

NICKNAME: *First State*

FLOWER: *Peach Blossom*

BIRD: *Blue Hen Chicken*

TREE: *American Holly*

SONG: *"Our Delaware"*

First of the original 13 states to ratify the Constitution, December 7, 1787

A FAMOUS DELAWAREAN: *Ryan Phillippe*

What are you when your alarm clock rings in Rehoboth?

Del-awake

How do they like their eggs in the capital of Delaware?

Dover-easy

Q: Did you know that Oliver Evans of Newport invented the automatic flour mill?

A: Did he make a lot of dough?

Where do royal lizards stay when visiting Delaware?

Newt Castle

He: Did you know that Delaware only has three counties—that's the fewest of any U.S. state!

She: Wow, it's so few you can COUNTY them on one hand!

BOY: What did Delaware?

GIRL: I don't know, Alaska

2ND BOY: I just found out—her New Jersey!

Q: How did you like your trip to **Delaware**?

A: It was DE-lightful

What do you call clothes you buy in Wilmington?

Dela-wear

Florida

ABBREVIATION: *FL*

STATE CAPITAL: *Tallahassee*

NICKNAME: *Sunshine State*

FLOWER: *Orange Blossom*

BIRD: *Mockingbird*

TREE: *Sabal Palmetto Palm*

SONG: *"Old Folks at Home"*

ENTERED UNION: *March 3, 1845*

A FAMOUS FLORIDIAN: *Gloria Estefan*

What is a **Floridian's** favorite cola?

Pensa-cola

What is a **Floridian's** favorite soda?

Sara-soda

Why do **Floridians** mix their orange juice with ocean water?

Because it's got more Vitamin Sea

Lazy Gator: Hey, do you want to knock off work early and go to the movies?

Busy Gator: I would, but I'm totally swamped!

Where do pigs like to visit in **Florida**?

My-hammy Beach

What's Santa Claus's favorite town in Florida?

Niceville

What footwear is waterproof and comes in sets of four?

Alligator shoes

What do you call someone who's been fired by NASA?

An astro-not

Georgia

ABBREVIATION: **GA**

STATE CAPITAL: *Atlanta*

NICKNAMES: *Empire State of the South,
Peach State*

FLOWER: *Cherokee Rose*

BIRD: *Brown Thrasher*

TREE: *Live Oak*

SONG: *"Georgia on My Mind"*

*Fourth of the 13 original states to ratify
the Constitution, January 2, 1788*

A FAMOUS GEORGIAN:
Martin Luther King, Jr.

Where in Georgia should you visit if you really like pickles or salad?

Cu-Cumberland Island

What Georgia landmark needs the world's largest toupee?

Brasstown Bald Mountain

Which Georgia military facility could use some cheering up?

Moody Air Force Base

Where can a mad scientist visit in Georgia, when he's not feeling like himself?

Jekyll Island

What did one **Georgia** fruit say to the other **Georgia** fruit?

You're a peach!

> *(Besides being called the Empire State of the South, Georgia is also known as the Peach State.)*

What word best describes Cordele, the watermelon capital of the world?

Seedy

Why does **Georgia's** state marine mammal never make a mistake?

Because it's the Right Whale

What do Atlanta fans do when their basketball team is playing?

Watch them like Hawks!

Hawaii

ABBREVIATION: *HI*

STATE CAPITAL: *Honolulu*

NICKNAME: *Aloha State*

FLOWER: *Yellow Hibiscus*

BIRD: *Hawaiian Goose*

TREE: *Kukui (Candlenut)*

SONG: *"Hawai'i Pono'i"*

ENTERED UNION: *August 21, 1959*

A FAMOUS HAWAIIAN: *Tia Carrere*

In Hawaii, how do they laugh at a joke that's just a little funny?

With a-low-ha

What do you call it when you see by the light of an erupting volcano?

A lava lamp

Q: **Did you know that Hawaiians only use the letters A, E, H, I, K, L, M, N, O, P, U, and W?**

A: **They must still be hungry after they eat alphabet soup!**

(The Hawaiian alphabet has so few letters because that's all that is required to spell every sound in the Hawaiian language.)

What do you call Hawaii's largest and youngest island?

The Big Baby

How does the volcano Kilauea Iki keep fit?

It stays active

Q: What comes after Waikiki?

A: X-kiki and Z-kiki?

What would you call dinner rolls made with Hawaiian flowers?

Hi-biscuits

What do you call it when you hang ten and then crash onto shore?

Surf and turf

Idaho

ABBREVIATION: *ID*

STATE CAPITAL: *Boise*

NICKNAME: *Gem State*

FLOWER: *Syringa*

BIRD: *Mountain Bluebird*

TREE: *White Pine*

SONG: *"Here We Have Idaho"*

ENTERED UNION: *July 3, 1890*

A FAMOUS IDAHOAN: *Sacagawea*

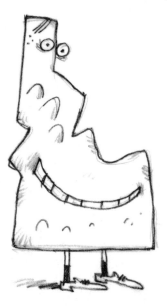

What Idaho town should ballerinas visit?

Grace

What part of your tongue enables you to sense the flavor of potatoes?

Your taste spuds

In Idaho, what's a baseball player's favorite town?

Ketchum

Which human-made geyser would be good to have when you're thirsty?

Soda Springs

Why do people love the Idaho ghost towns of Silver City, Yankee Fork, Gold Dredge, and Sierra Silver Mine?

Because they're boo-tiful

Q: Do you want to go to Anderson Dam for some fly fishing?

A: I guess, but last time I went, I didn't catch one fly

What do you call it when another state tries to pretend it is Idaho?

A fake ID

What would be a good name for a loud all-male singing group from Idaho's capital?

The Noisy Boise Boys

Illinois

ABBREVIATION: *IL*

STATE CAPITAL: *Springfield*

NICKNAMES: *Prairie State,
Land of Lincoln*

FLOWER: *Native Violet*

BIRD: *Cardinal*

TREE: *White Oak*

SONG: *"Illinois"*

ENTERED UNION: *December 3, 1818*

A FAMOUS ILLINOISAN:
Hillary Rodham Clinton

BOY: My report is on Abraham Lincoln.

TEACHER: The "L" is silent.

BOY: Okay, then my report is on Abraham Incoln.

Why do people from Chicago love chili so much?

It's the Windy City

Why are people from the Windy City so bashful?

Because it's Chi-town

What do you call a house between two other houses in the fields of Illinois?

Middle House on the Prairie

Q: What would you say if I repeated the word Peoria 100 times without stopping?

A: I'd say you were Illin-oying

Which part of Illinois sounds like a good place to stop for lunch?

Cook County

HE: Did you know that O'Hare Airport in Chicago is the world's busiest?

SHE: With all those jets flying overhead, it's a wonder they don't call the state Illi-NOISY!

Do you know what's strange about Chicago?

Chicago Cubs don't grow up to be Chicago Bears

Indiana

ABBREVIATION: *IN*

STATE CAPITAL: *Indianapolis*

NICKNAME: *Hoosier State*

FLOWER: *Peony*

BIRD: *Cardinal*

TREE: *Tulip Poplar*

SONG: *"On the Banks of the Wabash, Far Away"*

ENTERED UNION: *December 11, 1816*

A FAMOUS "HOOSIER": *David Letterman*

GIRL: Did you know Abe Lincoln moved to Indiana when he was seven?

BOY: Really?

GIRL: Honest!

In which Indiana town might you enter your houses through the chimney?

Santa Claus

WELCOME

What do you call 2,000 pounds of spring flowers in Indiana?

Blooming-ton

Why do cranky people feel at home in Indiana?

Because it's the crossroads of America

Ya Know What?

Peru, Indiana, was once called the "Circus Capital" of America.

Why do people like to kiss the state tree of Indiana?

Because it's the tu-lip tree

Knock Knock

Who's there?

Wabash

Wabash who?

Wabash yobour habands, plebease!

On which Indiana river should you be extra careful while boating?

Tippecanoe

My mother's sister just moved to Indiana.

Really? Hoosier aunt?

Iowa

ABBREVIATION: *IA*

STATE CAPITAL: *Des Moines*

NICKNAME: *Hawkeye State*

FLOWER: *Wild Rose*

BIRD: *Eastern Goldfinch*

TREE: *Oak*

SONG: *"The Song of Iowa"*

ENTERED UNION: *December 28, 1846*

A FAMOUS IOWAN: *Ashton Kutcher*

What is the favorite town of Iowa lawyers?

Sioux City

Which Iowa town should you visit if you don't like playing it straight?

Diagonal

Which town in Iowa is loved by tough guys everywhere?
Manly

Which Iowa town is perfect for pep squad members?

What Cheer

What do toddlers in Des Moines ask their parents for late at night?

A drink of Io-wa-wa

Where in **Iowa** should you go for a guaranteed laugh?

De Witt

Why should you never pet the **Iowa** state flower?

Because it's the wild rose

GIRL: Did you know that Iowa leads all U.S. states in egg production?

BOY: Wow, they should shell-abrate!

Kansas

ABBREVIATION: KS

STATE CAPITAL: Topeka

NICKNAME: Sunflower State

FLOWER: Native Sunflower

BIRD: Western Meadowlark

TREE: Cottonwood

SONG: "Home on the Range"

ENTERED UNION: January 29, 1861

**A FAMOUS KANSAN:
President Dwight D. Eisenhower**

Where in Kansas do they only drive one brand of car?

Dodge City

Where's the best place in Kansas to throw away your old shoes?

Boot Hill

What's the softest tree in the world?

The cottonwood

What did the cow say when the farmer caught him sleeping on his stove?

"I was feeling at home on the range!"

Which Kansas scientist might have been handy on Thanksgiving?

George Washington Carver

How did Kansans feel during the grasshopper plague of 1874?

Kind of jumpy

What did citizens call the town of Coffeyville after it was hit by a hailstone weighing more than one-and-a-half pounds?

Iced Coffeyville

What game do Kansans try to avoid?

Twister

Kentucky

ABBREVIATION: *KY*

STATE CAPITAL: *Frankfort*

NICKNAME: *Bluegrass State*

FLOWER: *Goldenrod*

BIRD: *Cardinal*

TREE: *Tulip Poplar*

SONG: *"My Old Kentucky Home"*

ENTERED UNION: *June 1, 1792*

A FAMOUS KENTUCKIAN: *Muhammad Ali*

When do people like to visit Bowling Green?

In their "spare" time

Which gymnastic event is the favorite of those who work at Fort Knox?

Vaulting

Where do citizens of **Kentucky's** capital hide their hot dogs?

At Frank Fort

Why do people love **Kentucky's** state tree so much?

Because it's very poplar

Q: Did you know Thomas Edison first exhibited the electric lightbulb in **Kentucky**?

A: No, thanks for illuminating me

HE: Did you know the Echo River is in Kentucky?

SHE: No, I didn't, idn't, idn't, idn't.

What do you call a mallard who finds a box of crackers in Lexington?

A lucky Kentucky ducky

What happens when people see horror movies in Bedford?

They Trimble with fear!

(Bedford is one of the towns in Trimble County, Kentucky.)

Ya Know What?

The song "Happy Birthday to You" was written in 1893 by two sisters from Louisville, Kentucky.

Louisiana

ABBREVIATION: *LA*

STATE CAPITAL: *Baton Rouge*

NICKNAME: *Pelican State*

FLOWER: *Magnolia*

BIRD: *Eastern Brown Pelican*

TREE: *Cypress*

SONG: *"Give Me Louisiana"*

ENTERED UNION: *April 30, 1812*

A FAMOUS LOUISIANAN: *Britney Spears*

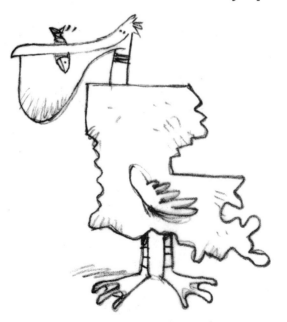

Why did the student ask to take all his tests in New Orleans?

Because it's the
Big Easy

Where in New Orleans does the money speak a different language?

The French Quarter

Why should you invite a Louisianan to your birthday party?

They might "bayou" something

(Bayou is a word used to describe a slow-moving river.)

What do Louisiana travelers say when they've already been to the North, South, and East?

Westwego

Ya Know What?

It's reported that in Louisiana, biting someone with false teeth is a more serious crime than biting someone with your own teeth.

Where in Louisiana should you visit if you like telling other people what to do?

Bossier City

What Cajun dish is less chewy than it sounds?

Gumbo

What kind of dance do felines like to do in Louisiana?

The Catahoula

How did you feel after you spent a day fishing in St. Bernard?

Dog-tired

Maine

ABBREVIATION: *ME*

STATE CAPITAL: *Augusta*

NICKNAME: *Pine Tree State*

FLOWER: *White Pine Cone and Tassel*

BIRD: *Chickadee*

TREE: *Eastern White Pine*

SONG: *"State of Maine Song"*

ENTERED UNION: *March 15, 1820*

A FAMOUS MAINER: *Liv Tyler*

What did the lobster say to the crab?

You're so shellfish

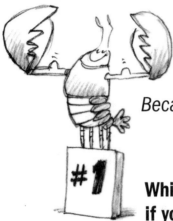

Why are Maine lobsters considered the best in the world?

Because they clawed their way to the top

Which Maine town should you visit if you're dirty?

Bath

Q: Did you know Maine grows and harvests 99% of the blueberries in this country?

A: Wow! They must be bushed!

How did the wasp propose to the Maine state insect?

"Honey bee mine forever!"

What does the Maine state tree order at Dairy Queen?

A pine cone

Where do you ski if you've got a sweet tooth?

Sugarloaf

BOY: Hey, this book says there was once a giant poet from Maine.

GIRL: A giant? Are you sure?

BOY: Well, it says here he was a Longfellow!

(Henry Wadsworth Longfellow was one of America's most famous poets. You should check him out!)

Maryland

ABBREVIATION: *MD*

STATE CAPITAL: *Annapolis*

NICKNAME: *Old Line State*

FLOWER: *Black-Eyed Susan*

BIRD: *Baltimore Oriole*

TREE: *White Oak*

SONG: *"Maryland, My Maryland"*

Seventh of the original 13 states to ratify the Constitution on April 28, 1788

A FAMOUS MARYLANDER:
Francis Scott Key

In Maryland, what do you make for an angry friend's birthday?

A crab cake

HE: I just visited the Babe Ruth Birthplace and Baseball Center in Baltimore.

SHE: Really? I didn't know that was his homer town!

Where do Maryland chiropractors like to hike?

Backbone Mountain

Where do university students like to picnic?

College Park

Which birds spend their days playing with bats?

The Baltimore Orioles

Where in **Maryland** is it hardest to mow the lawn?

Rockville

GIRL: Did you know the first school in the United States opened in Maryland in 1696?

BOY: Now I know who to blame!

Where do mountain goats most like to hang their laundry?

Mount Airy

Massachusetts

ABBREVIATION: *MA*

STATE CAPITAL: *Boston*

NICKNAME: *Bay State*

FLOWER: *Mayflower*

BIRD: *Chickadee*

TREE: *American Elm*

SONG: *"All Hail Massachusetts"*

Sixth of the original 13 states to ratify the Constitution on February 6, 1788

A FAMOUS NAME FROM MASSACHUSETTS:
Edgar Allan Poe

In what state do they most love gum?

Massa-chew-setts

What superhero protects the coastline of Massachusetts?

The Caped Cod

What did the pilgrims say when they landed on Plymouth Rock?

"Ouch!"

What do witches do when somebody gives them toy boats?

Salem

Why should the Boston Celtics players wear bibs?

They're always dribbling

(The game of basketball was invented in Springfield, Massachusetts.)

BOY: Did you know a man named Elias invented the sewing machine?

GIRL: Really, Howe?

(Elias Howe is credited with inventing the sewing machine.)

Q: What do you call the horse parked outside the silversmith shop?

A: Paul Revere's ride

What do April showers always bring in Massachusetts?

Mayflowers

Ya Know What?
Boston cream pie is the official dessert of the state of Massachusetts.

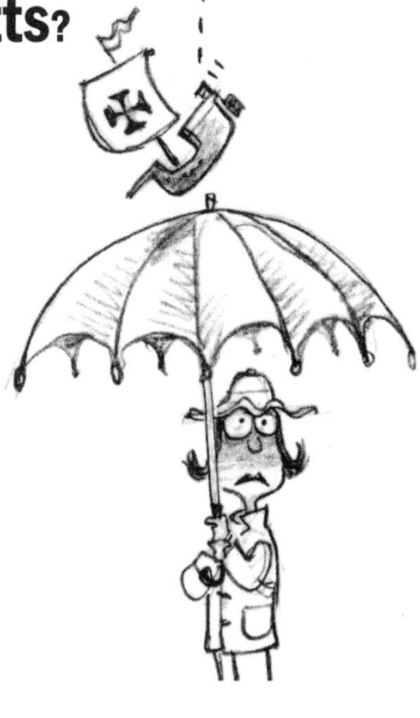

Michigan

ABBREVIATION: *MI*

STATE CAPITAL: *Lansing*

NICKNAME: *Great Lakes State*

FLOWER: *Apple Blossom*

BIRD: *Robin*

TREE: *White Pine*

SONG: *"Michigan, My Michigan"*

ENTERED UNION: *January 26, 1837*

A FAMOUS MICHIGANDER: *Madonna*

What did one Great Lake say when he kept running into another one?

Oh, that's just Erie!

If a knight on horseback moved to Michigan, where do you think he'd live?

Lansing

If the knight couldn't find a place in Lansing, where else could he try?

Battle Creek

She: Is it true that your grandfather takes care of animals in Michigan?

He: Yes, he's a KalamaZOOkeeper.

What would the Great Lakes be called if they weren't so spectacular?

The Just Okay Lakes

What do you call it when you visit the Great Lake State for a second time?

Mich-again

What do you call someone from Detroit who talks a lot?

Motor City Mouth

What do wolves gargle with?

Wolverine

(Michigan is still sometimes called "The Wolverine State" although wolverines no longer roam there.)

Minnesota

ABBREVIATION: *MN*

STATE CAPITAL: *St. Paul*

NICKNAME: *Gopher State*

FLOWER: *Pink and White Lady's Slipper*

BIRD: *Common Loon*

TREE: *Red Pine*

SONG: *"Hail! Minnesota"*

ENTERED UNION: *May 11, 1858*

A FAMOUS MINNESOTAN: *Prince*

What do you order when you're just a little thirsty in Rochester?

A mini-soda

A bird stood before a judge, waiting to hear his punishment. The judge said, "Before I begin, I have to ask: Are you some kind of a cuckoo?" The bird answered, **"No, but I am a Common Loon."**

What did the Minnesota weatherman sing for his forecast?

"Hail, Minnesota!"

What legendary Minnesota woodsman sounds like he had foot problems?

Paul Bunyan

Ya Know What?

The skyway system in Minneapolis, Minnesota, connects 52 blocks of downtown—you can do all your errands without your feet touching the street.

What do you call it when you're trampled during a big sale in Bloomington?

The Maul of America

(The Mall of America in Bloomington is equal in length to 78 football fields.)

Why aren't you allowed to scale the walls of the Metrodome?

Because it's climb-it controlled

What do you eat with in Minnesota when you're really, really hungry?

The Big Fork

Girl: Have you ever visited the U.S. Hockey Hall of Fame in Eveleth?

Boy: No, but it's my goal!

Mississippi

ABBREVIATION: MS

STATE CAPITAL: Jackson

NICKNAME: Magnolia State

FLOWER: Magnolia

BIRD: Mockingbird

TREE: Magnolia

SONG: "Go, Mississippi!"

ENTERED UNION: December 10, 1817

**A FAMOUS MISSISSIPPIAN:
Oprah Winfrey**

Why can the Mississippi River see so well?

Because it has five "I's"

Why did Mississippi feel unwanted?

Because people kept singing "Go, Mississippi!"

Which town can tell you if "he loves you" or "he loves you not"?

Petal

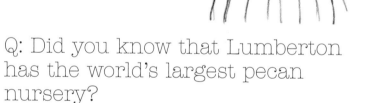

Q: Did you know that Lumberton has the world's largest pecan nursery?

A: I'd heard that, but I just can't imagine changing all those tiny little diapers.

Who is Mississippi married to?

Mr. Ippi

What did Elvis Presley say when he found out he was from the same state as the International Checkers Hall of Fame?

King me!

How cold was it last night in **Mississippi**?

Tupelo-zero!

What do you call it when **Mississippi** farmers cry because their crops aren't good?

A cotton bawl

Missouri

ABBREVIATION: **MO**

STATE CAPITAL: **Jefferson City**

NICKNAME: **Show Me State**

FLOWER: **Hawthorn**

BIRD: **Bluebird**

TREE: **Dogwood**

SONG: **"Missouri Waltz"**

ENTERED UNION: **August 10, 1821**

A FAMOUS MISSOURIAN: **Walt Disney**

Why do people from this state love it when folks come to visit?

Because Missouri loves company

What do you call two people dueling beneath St. Louis's most famous landmark?

Arch rivals

What would happen if Missouri were the footwear capital of the United States?

It would be called the Shoe-Me State

Which tree has more bite and bark?

The dogwood

BEWARE OF TREE

What's the biggest tollbooth in the United States?

Missouri: It's the gateway to the west

Which bird looks like it's been holding it's breath?
The blue bird

What kind of bird wears a glove?

A St. Louis Cardinal

Did you know that the first ice-cream cone was sold in St. Louis in 1904?

What a scoop!

Ya Know What?

Missouri was named for a tribe of Indians whose name meant "town of the large canoes."

Montana

ABBREVIATION: *MT*

STATE CAPITAL: *Helena*

NICKNAME: *Treasure State*

FLOWER: *Bitterroot*

BIRD: *Western Meadowlark*

TREE: *Ponderosa Pine*

SONG: *"Montana"*

ENTERED UNION: *November 8, 1889*

A FAMOUS MONTANAN: *Evel Knievel*

What dessert did they serve at Little Big Horn?

Custer'd Pie

Why did General Custer walk with a limp?

He had a Little Big Corn

Why is there a lot of wide-open space in Montana?

Because it's MT

Who's the favorite football player of the people in this state?

Joe Montana (What, you thought we were going to say Tiki Barber?)

What did the buffalo mother say to her child before he left for school?

Bison

Why is Humpty Dumpty terrified of Montana?

Because of Great Falls

What did Oula's boyfriend say when she went out of town?

I Missoula!

Which two super-explorers first searched Montana faster than a speeding bullet?

Lewis and Clark Kent

Nebraska

ABBREVIATION: *NE*

STATE CAPITAL: *Lincoln*

NICKNAME: *Cornhusker State*

FLOWER: *Goldenrod*

BIRD: *Western Meadowlark*

TREE: *Cottonwood*

SONG: *"Beautiful Nebraska"*

ENTERED UNION: *March 1, 1867*

A FAMOUS NEBRASKAN:
President Gerald Ford

Where do the funniest people in Nebraska live?

Oma-ha-ha-ha

What do a penny, Ford Motor cars, and Nebraska all have in common?

They all have a Lincoln

What town do Nebraska picnic pests run off to when they want to get married?

Antelope

What happens when you find poison ivy in Hastings?

Neb-rash-ka

What did the Nebraska-born kid say when his mother told a funny joke?

O-ma-ha!

Which Nebraska landmark reminds Santa of his favorite kind of music?

Chimney Rock

What's the happiest town in Nebraska?

Wahoo

What do you get when you buy a Bison with your credit card?

Buffalo Bill

Nevada

ABBREVIATION: **NV**

STATE CAPITAL: **Carson City**

NICKNAMES: **Silver State, Sagebrush State, Battle Born State**

FLOWER: **Sagebrush**

BIRD: **Mountain Bluebird**

TREE: **Bristlecone Pine**

SONG: **"Home Means Nevada"**

ENTERED UNION: **October 31, 1864**

A FAMOUS NEVADAN: **Andre Agassi**

Why do Nevada residents love Boulder City?

It rocks

Where does Santa Claus stay when he visits Nevada?

LAKE TAHOE-HO-HO

What do you call a skeleton in a dress?

Death Valley girl

Where do all the mummies in Nevada like to go swimming?

PYRAMID LAKE

Which Nevada town are you in when you accidentally cross two live wires?

Sparks

What do you call it when someone from Nevada turns you down once, then a second time?

Re-no

In what town do they tell a lot of jokes?

Laugh-lin

SHE: My uncle in Nevada sure talks a lot

HE: You should send him to Gabbs!

New Hampshire

ABBREVIATION: *NH*

STATE CAPITAL: *Concord*

NICKNAME: *Granite State*

FLOWER: *Purple Lilac*

BIRD: *Purple Finch*

TREE: *White Birch*

SONG: *"Old New Hampshire"*

ENTERED UNION: *June 21, 1788*

A FAMOUS NEW HAMPSHIRITE: *Adam Sandler*

When your pet rodent dies in this state, what should you get?

A New Hampster

How could you tell the Old Man of the Mountain was so serious?

Because he was stone-faced

Why do people go to visit the Flume while in New Hampshire?

Because it's gorge-ous

Why do people love New Hampshire?

It's a Keene State

In 1998, skiing became
the official sport of
New Hampshire...

**and it's all been
downhill since then!**

Why was the foolish man excited about the New Hampshire presidential primary?

He thought he'd be getting candied dates

What's the New Hampshire hairdressers' state motto?

Live Free or Dye

Hey, do you want to go to New Hampshire for some fly-fishing with me?

Okay, I'll fish for flies, but I won't eat them

Ya Know What?
The first free, tax-supported public library in U.S. history was opened in New Hampshire back in 1833.

New Jersey

ABBREVIATION: *NJ*

STATE CAPITAL: *Trenton*

NICKNAME: *Garden State*

FLOWER: *Violet*

BIRD: *Eastern Goldfinch*

TREE: *Red Oak*

SONGS: *"New Jersey Loyalty,"*
"I'm From New Jersey"

ENTERED UNION: *December 18, 1787*

A FAMOUS NEW JERSEYAN: *Jon Bon Jovi*

Why are New Jersey residents like that beanstalk kid Jack?

They get to watch the Giants play

Where is a wildebeest's favorite place to live?

Gnu Jersey

What did people say about Thomas Edison after he invented the phonograph and electric light?

What a record achievement by a bright guy

Where is a cow's favorite place to live?
Moo Jersey

Q: **I just visited New Jersey's spoon museum. It had more than 5,000 spoons on display. Guess what they said at the admission counter.**

A: **Five bucks...fork it over!**

New Jersey's state animal is the horse. So when you move there, they say, "Welcome to the **neighhhh**borhood."

What do you call it when you take a stroll in Atlantic City because there's nothing else to do?

A bored-walk

What does Santa yell when he lands in New Jersey, the Garden State?

Hoe, hoe, hoe

Hoe! Hoe! Hoe!

New Mexico

ABBREVIATION: **NM**

STATE CAPITAL: **Santa Fe**

NICKNAME: **Land of Enchantment**

FLOWER: **Yucca Flower**

BIRD: **Roadrunner**

TREE: **Piñon**

SONG: **"O Fair New Mexico"**

ENTERED UNION: **January 6, 1912**

A FAMOUS NEW MEXICAN: **Demi Moore**

What did the boy say when he tasted the official state flower?

Yucca!

GIRL: How do you start your auto in New Mexico's largest city?

BOY: How?

GIRL: With an Albu-car-key

SAME GIRL: What do you bake with chips in New Mexico's largest city?

SAME BOY: What?

SAME GIRL: An Albu-cookie

Which New Mexico town should never have an energy crisis?

Pep

SHE: Did I tell you…I'm taking a trip on the river to visit my relatives!

HE: Who are you seeing?

SHE: My Rio Grande-ma

HE: Do you want to come with me to hear, "Baa baa boing"?

SHE: Where are you going?

HE: Sheep Springs

Did you really tour all the caves at Carlsbad Cavern?

Yes, I saw the hole thing!

Where's a good place for cowboys to live in New Mexico?

Gallup!

New York

ABBREVIATION: **NY**

STATE CAPITAL: **Albany**

NICKNAME: **Empire State**

FLOWER: **Rose**

BIRD: **Bluebird**

TREE: **Sugar Maple**

SONG: **"I Love New York"**

ENTERED UNION: **July 26, 1788**

A FAMOUS NEW YORKER: **Jerry Seinfeld**

Where do baseball ball-and-strike callers stay while in New York City?

The Umpire State Building

Did you get a lot of rain in
New York this week?

**Are you kidding?
From now on, we're calling it
the Big Apple Juice!**

What happened when you forgot to wake up the Radio City dancers while they were sunbathing?

I saw the Rockettes' red glare

If CorningWare is made in Corning, New York ... what do you think they make in Fort Drum?

A lot of noise

Ya Know What?
The New York City subway system has 722 miles of track.
(If you straightened it out, it would stretch all the way to Indianapolis, Indiana!)

Which part of New York City do mathematicians like best?

Times Square

Why are the New York Rangers good role models?

Because they're very goal-oriented

Why is it New Year's Eve all season long at Shea Stadium?

Because they drop the ball there every day!

Where are you likely to find felines who can juggle and type?

In the Cat-skill Mountains

North Carolina

ABBREVIATION: *NC*

STATE CAPITAL: *Raleigh*

NICKNAME: *Tar Heel State*

FLOWER: *American Dogwood*

BIRD: *Cardinal*

TREE: *Longleaf Pine*

SONG: *"The Old North State"*

ENTERED UNION: *November 21, 1789*

FAMOUS NORTH CAROLINIAN: *Michael Jordan*

Are you aware that the sweet potato is North Carolina's state vegetable?

Yes, I yam

Is it far from Winston to Salem?

No, it's just a short dash between Winston-Salem

Teacher: Andrew, what's the capital of North Carolina?

Andrew: It has two

Teacher: What do you mean it has two?

Andrew: Capital N and Capital C

He: North Carolina has a beautiful state capital

She: Really?

He: No, Raleigh

It says here that Wilbur and Orville made their first successful flight at Kitty Hawk in North Carolina...

Is that Wright?

Would you like to smell the state flower of North Carolina?

No, but my dogwood

SNIFF
SNIFF

Why did the North Carolinian's shoe stick in the street?

Because it's the Tar Heel State!

What do you call a person who wishes they lived east of Guilford, North Carolina?

Greensboro with envy

107

North Dakota

ABBREVIATION: ND

STATE CAPITAL: Bismarck

NICKNAMES: Peace Garden State, Flickertail State, Sioux State

FLOWER: Wild Prairie Rose

BIRD: Western Meadowlark

TREE: American Elm

SONG: "North Dakota Hymn"

ENTERED UNION: November 2, 1889

A FAMOUS NORTH DAKOTAN: Baseball's Darin Erstad

How did you answer the test question about the capital of North Dakota?

None of your Bismarck!

Do you want to walk to Fargo?

Yes, but after an hour I have to Farcomeback

Which North Dakota town sounds like it's been hit by lightning?

Zap!

Q: While in North Dakota, have you ever seen Washburn?

A: Once, when I left it in the dryer too long

He: Did you know the Turtle Mountains are in North Dakota?

She: Yes, our teacher tortoise that today

Lost Tourist: Excuse me, how do I get to Grand Forks?

Boy: Make a left at the spoon in the road

Same Lost Tourist (the next day): Excuse me, how do I get to Stump Lake?

Same Boy: Ya got me!

Same Lost Tourist (later that day): Excuse me, can you show me the way to Steele?

Same Boy: No...and you should be ashamed of yourself!

Ya Know What?
"Dakota" is the Sioux Indian word for friend.

Ohio

ABBREVIATION: *OH*

STATE CAPITAL: *Columbus*

NICKNAME: *Buckeye State*

FLOWER: *Scarlet Carnation*

BIRD: *Cardinal*

TREE: *Buckeye*

SONG: *"Beautiful Ohio"*

ENTERED UNION: *March 1, 1803*

A FAMOUS OHIOAN: *Toni Morrison*

How can you visit Chicago, Kansas, and Boston without ever leaving Cleveland?

Go to the Rock and Roll Hall of Fame

Why should you never pay $2 for an optical exam in Ohio?

Because it's the Buck-eye State

Would you like to visit the Pro Football Hall of Fame?

Sorry, I Canton

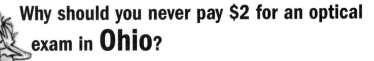

(Canton is the home of the Pro Football Hall of Fame.)

Boy: Neil Armstrong, the first man to walk on the moon, is from the Ohio town of Wapakaneta!

Girl: No wonder he went to the moon—it's easier to pronounce!

Q: Why do people say that Ohio is the friendliest state?

A: It's the only one with "hi" in the middle of its name!

Where are the happiest waitresses in Ohio?

Tipp City

My doctor is the greatest!
How come?
I was in Painesville, and he got me to Mount Healthy!
(Both are towns in Ohio!)

What makes you say that the best animal trainers in the world are in Cincinnati?

I saw a group of Bengals playing football!

Oklahoma

ABBREVIATION: *OK*

STATE CAPITAL: *Oklahoma City*

NICKNAME: *Sooner State*

FLOWER: *Mistletoe*

BIRD: *Scissor-Tailed Flycatcher*

TREE: *Redbud*

SONG: *"Oklahoma!"*

ENTERED UNION: *November 16, 1907*

A FAMOUS OKLAHOMAN: *Brad Pitt*

Do you mind if I abbreviate Oklahoma?

It's OK with me

I have a cousin who lives in Disney, Oklahoma.

Me, too—it's a small world after all!

Were you living in Oklahoma when they filmed scenes for the movie <u>Twister</u>?

Yes, I think they should have called it
<u>Gone with the Wind</u>

SHE: My friend in Oklahoma always says his town is the best

HE: He must live in Braggs!

If you rearrange the letters in the word **OKLAHOMA**, it spells **LOOK—A HAM**!

That has nothing to do with the state, but we thought you should know.

Ya Know What?

Oklahoma!, the Rodgers and Hammerstein classic, is the longest-running Broadway musical with a state name in its title.

BOY: When are you going back to Oklahoma?

GIRL: The Sooner, the better

Q: Which **Oklahoma** town do people ask, and ask, and ask to see?

A: Beggs

How do you get to the Cowboy Hall of Fame?

Steer

What do you call it when a pilot is in a hurry to set his plane down in Oklahoma?

A "Land Rush"

Oregon

ABBREVIATION: *OR*

STATE CAPITAL: *Salem*

NICKNAME: *Beaver State*

FLOWER: *Oregon Grape*

BIRD: *Western Meadowlark*

TREE: *Douglas Fir*

SONG: *"Oregon, My Oregon"*

ENTERED UNION: *February 14, 1859*

A FAMOUS OREGONIAN: *Beverly Cleary*

What is a Salem resident's favorite spice?

Oregon-o

BOY: According to this map, there is a town in Oregon called Zigzag

GIRL: Are you sure you've got that straight?

What does an auctioneer in Portland yell after the highest bid has been received?

Going, going, Ore-gone!

Would you do me a favor and mail this package to zip code 97140?

Sherwood

Which Oregon ski resort has a name that doesn't sound like a great place for honeymooners?

Mt. Bachelor

SHE: What makes you say people who send mail to Medford can't mind up their minds?

HE: The address on every envelope ends in OR!

Where in Oregon is it impossible to find a needle?

Haystack Rock

Where is a good place to go when your head is cold?

Mt. Hood

Pennsylvania

ABBREVIATION: *PA*

STATE CAPITAL: *Harrisburg*

NICKNAME: *Keystone State*

FLOWER: *Mountain Laurel*

BIRD: *Ruffed Grouse*

TREE: *Eastern Hemlock*

SONG: *"Pennsylvania"*

ENTERED UNION: *December 12, 1787*

A FAMOUS PENNSYLVANIAN: *Bill Cosby*

Q: What happens when a boy from Scranton is done with his Massachusetts vacation?

A: He leaves MA and returns to PA

Since **Pennsylvania** leads all states in pretzel making, what's their favorite dance?

The Twist

What's a good way to annoy your sister in Pennsylvaia?

Poconos

How can you tell Philadelphia is a funny city?

Even the Liberty Bell is cracking up

HE: I just got back from Pennsylvania

SHE: Did you stop in Ringing Hill?

HE: Yes, but there was no answer

Why is it so amazing to watch **Pennsylvania** sports teams?

Because you can see an Eagle run for a touchdown and a Penguin score a goal

What kind of Philadelphia horse can play baseball?

A Phillie

Where do peaches and plums attend college in Pennsylvania?

Pitt

Rhode Island

ABBREVIATION: *RI*

STATE CAPITAL: *Providence*

NICKNAMES: *Ocean State, Little Rhody*

FLOWER: *Violet*

BIRD: *Rhode Island Red*

TREE: *Red Maple*

SONG: *"Rhode Island's It For Me"*

ENTERED UNION: *May 29, 1790*

A FAMOUS RHODE ISLANDER:
George M. Cohan (of "Yankee Doodle" fame)

What's Rhode Island's favorite flavor of ice cream?

Rhocky Rhode

Where is a toddler's favorite place to go in Rhode Island?

Block Island

Why was the man so happy living 10 miles west of Providence?

He was well-Scituated

(The Scituate Reservoir provides water to most of Rhode Island.)

Q: Why do they call this state Little Rhody?

A: Because Little Boulevardy was too hard to say

What Rhode Island town is the favorite of all cats and dogs?

Paw-tucket

What do you call it when a Rhode Island Red is eating lettuce?

Chicken Salad

Which Rhode Island town is BUZZING with electricity?

Woon-socket

What do you call this state when you reach it by paddling your own boat?

Rowed Island

South Carolina

ABBREVIATION: **SC**

STATE CAPITAL: **Columbia**

NICKNAME: **Palmetto State**

FLOWER: **Yellow Jessamine**

BIRD: **Great Carolina Wren**

TREE: **Cabbage Palmetto**

SONG: **"Carolina"**

ENTERED UNION: **May 23, 1788**

A FAMOUS CAROLINIAN: **Jesse Jackson**

Which South Carolina town sounds like it needs some courage?

Coward

What does the state bird of South Carolina do when it wants to live in a new tree?

It Wren-ts one

Which town in South Carolina sounds like it's always sunny?

Merriwether

Has your kitty ever been to Cat Island, South Carolina?

Nine Times

(Both Cat Island and Nine Times are places to visit there.)

Ya Know What?
The East Coast Hockey League team in Greenville, South Carolina, is called the Grrrowl.

(They should change the name of the town to Grrreenville!)

Where should heifers and calves visit in South Carolina when they want to write a letter?

The Cowpens Museum

What could you say about the river that flows through the middle of South Carolina?

It's Wateree

GIRL: What would you call the water monster that legend says is living in Lake Murray?

BOY: I wouldn't call it

Why are baskets made in Mount Pleasant so tasty?

Because they're made from Sweetgrass

South Dakota

ABBREVIATION: *SD*

STATE CAPITAL: *Pierre*

NICKNAMES: *Mt. Rushmore State, Coyote State*

FLOWER: *American Pasqueflower*

BIRD: *Ring-Necked Pheasant*

TREE: *Black Hills Spruce*

SONG: *"Hail! South Dakota"*

ENTERED UNION: *November 2, 1889*

A FAMOUS SOUTH DAKOTAN: *Tom Brokaw*

Which comedian should be enshrined on Mount Rushmore?

Chris Rock

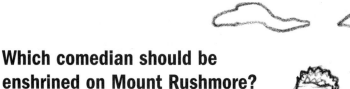

What's the best road for an acupuncturist to take in South Dakota?

Needles Highway

What did South Dakota citizens think when sculptor Gutzon Borglum took 14 years to carve a mountain with the faces of four famous presidents?

He should Rush-more!

GIRL: Are you going to the Mashed Potato Wrestling contest in Clark?

BOY: No, I'd rather see someone wrestle a roast turkey!

I have a friend who just moved to the town of White Owl.

Who?

Which South Dakota national park needs a time-out?

The Badlands

What did archaeologists in Hot Springs say when they found fossils of elephant relatives from the Ice Age?

What a mammoth discovery!

Why were paleontologists able to excavate a Tyrannosaurus Rex skeleton in South Dakota?

Because they had Faith!

(The town of Faith is well-known to dinosaur lovers—it's where one of the largest and best-preserved T. Rex specimens was found!)

Tennessee

ABBREVIATION: *TN*

STATE CAPITAL: *Nashville*

NICKNAME: *Volunteer State*

FLOWER: *Iris*

BIRD: *Mockingbird*

TREE: *Tulip Poplar*

SONGS: *"Tennessee Waltz," "Tennessee," "My Homeland, Tennessee," "Rocky Top," "When It's Iris Time in Tennessee"*

ENTERED UNION: *June 1, 1796*

A FAMOUS TENNESSEEAN: *Aretha Franklin*

What is the right thing to say if you accidentally bump into someone while at Dollywood?

"Parton me"

What's a frog's favorite place to hear country music?

The Grand Ole Hopry

How many fingers does the average Jackson resident have?

TENN

How come no one rings the doorbell near Norris Lake?

It's in **KnoX***ville*

How did they find out there were more horses in Shelby County than any other county in the United States?

A Gallop Poll

What does a **Tennessee** NFL player do if his mouth guard is too loose?

He Titans it

Why was Casey Jones, from Jackson, the world's most famous engineer?

He had excellent train-ing

BOY: I went to Reelfoot Lake and got a T-shirt that said "Turtle Capital of the World"!

GIRL: Really, how much did you shell out?

Texas

ABBREVIATION: *TX*

STATE CAPITAL: *Austin*

NICKNAME: *Lone Star State*

FLOWER: *Bluebonnet*

BIRD: *Mockingbird*

TREE: *Pecan*

SONG: *"Texas, Our Texas"*

ENTERED UNION: *December 29, 1845*

A FAMOUS TEXAN: *President George W. Bush*

What do Texans say when they want apple pie topped with ice cream?

"Remember the á la mode!"

Why are you wearing an oven mitt to visit Texas?

Because I heard the Panhandle was very hot!

Why did the Texas rancher punish his gushing oil?

It was being crude

Where is the best place to make a U-turn in Texas?

Big Bend

GIRL: Did you know that there's a Circus Museum in San Antonio?

BOY: Quit clowning around!

What does a hard-shelled mammal found in Texas like to rest its head on at night?

An armadillo pillow

Why did the Texas state bird make fun of the little boy?

It was a mockingbird

BOY: Did you know that Texas has more than sixteen million cattle?

GIRL: Holy Cow!

Utah

ABBREVIATION: *UT*

STATE CAPITAL: *Salt Lake City*

NICKNAME: *Beehive State*

FLOWER: *Sego Lily*

BIRD: *American Seagull*

TREE: *Blue Spruce*

SONG: *"Utah, We Love Thee"*

ENTERED UNION: *January 4, 1896*

A FAMOUS UTAHAN: *Football's Steve Young*

How was your trip to Hurricane, Utah?

Fine—I just blew into town!

Why did you go to Iron, Utah?

I had some pressing business!

What do you call someone who performs the national anthem before a Utah NBA game?

A Jazz singer

Why are Utah's mountains, on average, the tallest in the country?

Because they're in peak condition

GIRL: Did you know that Utah has the highest literacy rate in the whole nation?

BOY: That's terrible. I think they should litter less and read more!

Ya Know What?

Utah got its name from the Ute Tribe, meaning "people of the mountains."

When does water make you thirstier when you drink it?

When it comes from the Great Salt Lake

BOY: Did you know that Levan is right in the middle of Utah? And that it's actually "Navel" spelled backward!

GIRL: How appropriate. Hey, it's better than calling the place "ylleb nottub"!

"LEVAN"

What did the Utah skier say when she fell face-first into the snow?

"I'm just powdering my nose!"

Vermont

ABBREVIATION: *VT*

STATE CAPITAL: *Montpelier*

NICKNAME: *Green Mountain State*

FLOWER: *Red Clover*

BIRD: *Hermit Thrush*

TREE: *Sugar Maple*

SONG: *"Hail, Vermont"*

ENTERED UNION: *March 4, 1791*

A FAMOUS VERMONTER: *President Calvin Coolidge*

Why should you cover your head when you sing this state's song?

Because it's "Hail, *Vermont*"

What do you call someone who tries to sneak into a Vermont basketry festival?

A Stowe-away

Have you ever been to a Vermont town called Derby?

Not off the top of my head!

HE: I never realized that the state tree of Vermont is the Sugar Maple

SHE: What a sap!

Did you hear they're having a heat wave in Mount Snow?

Really?

Yes, now it's called Mount Slush!

Why does Montpelier produce the most maple syrup in the United States?

Because it sells like hotcakes

Why did your family just move to Victory, **Vermont?**

We figure we can't lose there

How did you enjoy your trip to Button Bay Park?

It was fasten-ating

Virginia

ABBREVIATION: **VA**

STATE CAPITAL: *Richmond*

NICKNAME: *Old Dominion*

FLOWER: *Dogwood*

BIRD: *Cardinal*

TREE: *Dogwood*

SONG: *"Carry Me Back to Old Virginny"*

ENTERED UNION: *June 25, 1788*

A FAMOUS VIRGINIAN: *Booker T. Washington*

What happens when a Virginia river is full?

It gets a Potomac-ache!

What should you do if you're paddling a canoe and your elm branch breaks?

Roanoke

HE: Doing research on Virginia has been fascinating! Do you realize that the first marriage ceremony in Virginia was held in 1609, and that rice was first imported there in 1647?

SHE: That's terrible! They had to go 38 years without having anything to throw at weddings!

In which Virginia town do the residents always know the scoop?

Newport News

Ya Know What?

It's a silly law, but...hens are not allowed to lay eggs in Norfolk, Virginia, before 8:00 in the morning and after 4:00 in the afternoon. (What a yolk!)

DAUGHTER: Did you know George Washington was born in Virginia?

MOTHER: Really?

DAUGHTER: I cannot tell a lie

In which **Virginia** town are there always three sides to every story?

Triangle

BOY: Will you tell me what kind of animal has been roaming on Assateague Island for centuries?

GIRL: Wild horses couldn't drag it out of me

What do you call somebody who refuses to get off the stage in Portsmouth?

*A **Virginia** Ham*

TAP!
TAPPITY TAP! TAP
TAP!
TAP!
TAP
TAPPITY
TAP

Washington

ABBREVIATION: **WA**

STATE CAPITAL: **Olympia**

NICKNAME: **Evergreen State**

FLOWER: **Western Rhododendron**

BIRD: **Willow Goldfinch**

TREE: **Western Hemlock**

SONG: **"Washington, My Home"**

ENTERED UNION: **November 11, 1889**

A FAMOUS WASHINGTONIAN: **Bill Gates**

Why doesn't fruit ripen in **Washington?**

It's the Evergreen State

Which **Washington** city sounds like they run up big phone bills?

Yakima

HE: Did you know that Washington is the only state to be named for a U.S. president?

SHE: Oh, yeah? What about Herbert Hoo-Vermont?

What do you call 2,000 pounds of laundry in Everett?

A Washing-ton

Do you want to go to Mt. Saint Helens?

Yes, I'd **lava** *to see it!*

What do many homes
in Washington have
on their floors?

Walla-to-Walla carpeting

Why can't you tell me the way to Concrete,
Washington?

It's hard

BOY: I was just stuck in
the northwest corner of
Washington. And do you know
what I found out?

SHE: What?

BOY: Cape Flattery will get
you nowhere!

West Virginia

ABBREVIATION: *WV*

STATE CAPITAL: *Charleston*

NICKNAME: *Mountain State*

FLOWER: *Big Rhododendron*

BIRD: *Cardinal*

TREE: *Sugar Maple*

SONGS: *"West Virginia, My Sweet Home," "The West Virginia Hills," "This is My West Virginia"*

ENTERED UNION: *June 20, 1863*

A FAMOUS WEST VIRGINIAN: *Chuck Yeager*

Does everyone in West Virginia have to remember the state bird?

Yes, it's a cardinal rule

HE: Although more than 7,000 people live in Calhoun County, West Virginia, there are no traffic lights in the whole county.

SHE: There's just no stopping those people!

Which county do long-haired West Virginians never visit?

Barbour

HE: Hide me! I'm being chased through the mountains!

SHE: I don't see anyone.

HE: Well, I'm far ahead right now, but they're Alleghening on me!

Ya Know What?

West Virginia's capital was originally Wheeling. For a brief while in the 1870s, it was changed to Charleston, then back to Wheeling, then back to Charleston.

FATHER: Did you know **West Virginia**'s state motto is "Mountaineers Are Always Free"?

SON: No—but that's good news, because I was saving my allowance to buy one

Did you know there's a town in West Virginia called Prosperity?

That's a rich one!

What did the owner of Coal House, a house entirely made from coal, say?

"It's all mine!"

Where could you find an American pioneer in West Virginia?

In the Daniel Boone-docks

Wisconsin

ABBREVIATION: *WI*

STATE CAPITAL: *Madison*

NICKNAMES: *Badger State, America's Dairyland*

FLOWER: *Wood Violet*

BIRD: *Robin*

TREE: *Sugar Maple*

SONG: *"On, Wisconsin"*

ENTERED UNION: *May 29, 1848*

A FAMOUS WISCONSINITE: *Harry Houdini*

HE: Green Bay Packers fans call themselves Cheeseheads

SHE: Maybe they think they're living in Swissconsin!

How do kids in Eau Claire do so well on school tests?

They Wisconsin-trate

Which Wisconsin town sounds like a good place to spend Halloween?

Bara **Boo**

HE: Did you know the Hamburger Hall of Fame is in Seymour, Wisconsin?

SHE: Wow, I'd better tell my friend Patty!

What kind of clothes do people wear when they do the Wisconsin state dance?

Polka-dotted!

(There are more than a dozen Polka events every year in Wisconsin!)

Q: Why did your family move to Brown Deer?

A: We wanted to save a few bucks!

Ya Know What?

The Ringling Brothers performed their first show in Wisconsin more than 130 years ago!

(Back then it was only the greatest show in town!)

Boy in Sheboygan: **Did you know that my town is the Bratwurst Capital of the World?**

Girl in Madison: **That's nothing. My brother is the wurst brat in the world!**

Do you want to read my report on Bloomer, Wisconsin—the Jump Rope Capital of the World?

I'd rather skip it

Wyoming

ABBREVIATION: **WY**

STATE CAPITAL: **Cheyenne**

NICKNAMES: **Equality State, Cowboy State**

FLOWER: **Indian Paintbrush**

BIRD: **Western Meadowlark**

TREE: **Cottonwood**

SONG: **"Wyoming"**

ENTERED UNION: **July 10, 1890**

A FAMOUS WYOMINGITE: **Jackson Pollock**

Ya Know What?

Wyoming is one of the top 10 states in terms of size, but it has the lowest population of all.

What's the best thing to do at a party in Cheyenne?

Wyo-mingle

Are you meeting the girls at Old Faithful?

Yes, the geyser there already

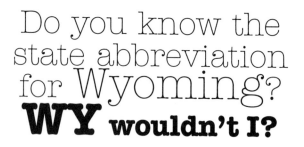

Do you know the state abbreviation for Wyoming? **WY** wouldn't I?

Did you break your foot while skiing in Wyoming?

Yes, I stepped in a Jackson Hole

Have you ever been to Basin, Wyoming?

No, I've washed my hands of that place!

HE: Did you know there's a place in Wyoming called Buffalo?

SHE: Never herd of it

SAME HE: Well, then, are you aware there's a place called Little Medicine?

SAME SHE: That's hard to swallow!

It's a silly law, but...
in **Wyoming** it is illegal
to take a picture of a rabbit
in the month of June!

A Word About the District of Columbia...

ATTENTION, WASHINGTON, D.C.:
You are not a state, but we
don't want to forget about you.
However, TV shows, radio reports, and
newspapers are always full of jokes
about what's going on in Washington...
so we thought we'd just salute you and say

have a nice day.

(That's a capitol idea!)